R-2904-ICJ

Educational Policymaking Through the Civil Justice System

Paul T. Hill and Doren L. Madey

1982

THE
INSTITUTE FOR
CIVIL JUSTICE

The Institute for Civil Justice

The Institute for Civil Justice, established within The Rand Corporation in 1979, performs independent, objective policy analysis and research on the American civil justice system. The Institute's principal purpose is to help make the civil justice system more efficient and more equitable by supplying policymakers with the results of empirically based, analytic research.

Rand is a private, non-profit institution, incorporated in 1948, which engages in nonpartisan research and analysis on problems of national security and the public welfare.

The Institute examines the policies that shape the civil justice system, the behavior of the people who participate in it, the operation of its institutions, and its effects on the nation's social and economic systems. Its work describes and assesses the current civil justice system; analyzes how this system has changed over time and may change in the future; evaluates recent and pending reforms in it; and carries out experiments and demonstrations. The Institute builds on a long tradition of Rand research characterized by an interdisciplinary, empirical approach to public policy issues and rigorous standards of quality, objectivity, and independence.

The Institute disseminates the results of its work widely to state and federal officials, legislators, and judges, to the business, consumer affairs, labor, legal, and research communities, and to the general public.

Board of Overseers

CHAUNCEY J. MEDBERRY, III, *Chairman of the Board, Bank of America (retired); Chairman of the Board of Overseers, The Institute for Civil Justice*

KENNETH J. ARROW, *The Joan Kenney Professor of Economics and Professor of Operations Research, Stanford University*

WILLIAM O. BAILEY, *President, Aetna Life and Casualty Company*

ARCHIE R. BOE, *President, Sears Roebuck & Company*

GUIDO CALABRESI, *Sterling Professor of Law, Yale Law School*

RICHARD P. COOLEY, *Chairman and Chief Executive Officer, Wells Fargo Bank and Wells Fargo & Company*

THOMAS R. DONAHUE, *Secretary-Treasurer, AFL-CIO*

W. RICHARD GOODWIN, *President and Chief Executive, Hughes Capital Corporation*

SHIRLEY M. HUFSTEDLER, *Attorney, Hufstedler, Miller, Carlson & Beardsley; former U.S. Circuit Judge; former Secretary, U.S. Department of Education*

JOHN A. LOVE, *Chairman, President and Chief Executive Officer, Ideal Basic Industries; former Governor of Colorado*

LAURENCE E. LYNN, JR., *Professor of Public Policy, John F. Kennedy School of Government, Harvard University*

ROBERT H. MALOTT, *Chairman and Chief Executive Officer, FMC Corporation*

EDWARD J. NOHA, *Chairman and Chief Executive Officer, CNA Insurance Companies*

WILLIAM B. SCHWARTZ, *Vannevar Bush University Professor and Professor of Medicine, Tufts University*

ELEANOR B. SHELDON, *former President, Social Science Research Council*

GUSTAVE H. SHUBERT, *Senior Vice President, The Rand Corporation; Director, The Institute for Civil Justice*

JUSTIN A. STANLEY, *Partner, Mayer, Brown & Platt; former President, American Bar Association*

POTTER STEWART, *Associate Justice, United States Supreme Court, retired (Will join the Board of Overseers, March 1983.)*

WARD WAGNER, JR., *Partner, Cone, Owen, Wagner, Nugent, Johnson, Hazouri & Roth; former President, The Association of Trial Lawyers of America*

ROBERT B. WILCOX, *President, Property-Casualty Insurance Council*

SANDRA L. WILLETT, *Executive Vice President, National Consumers League*

MARGARET BUSH WILSON, *Partner, Wilson, Smith and McCullin; Chairman of the NAACP National Board of Directors*

PAUL S. WISE, *President, Alliance of American Insurers*

LEONARD WOODCOCK, *Adjunct Professor of Political Science, University of Michigan; President Emeritus, United Auto Workers; former U.S. Ambassador to the People's Republic of China*

HONORARY MEMBERS

IRVING A. BLUESTONE, *Professor of Labor Studies, Wayne State University; former Vice President, United Auto Workers*

EDWARD H. LEVI, *Glen A. Lloyd Distinguished Service Professor, School of Law, University of Chicago; former Attorney General of the United States*

SAMUEL R. PIERCE, JR., *Secretary, U.S. Department of Housing and Urban Development*

DONALD H. RUMSFELD, *President and Chief Executive Officer, G.D. Searle & Company*

CHARLES J. ZWICK, *President and Chief Executive Officer, Southeast Banking Corporation; former Director of the U.S. Bureau of the Budget*

Foreword

Perhaps the most enduring of the cluster of policy concepts often associated with the "Great Society" programs of the 1960s is the principle that certain individuals are entitled to certain social, educational, and income-maintenance services as a matter of right, regardless of what the vindication of these rights may cost. This is the principle that underlies Medicare, Medicaid, and many less prominent programs that emerged in that era.

During the 1970s, the entitlement principle was sometimes combined with the proposition that the way to fulfill these rights was not necessarily to explain and interpret the laws that established them in reams of detailed regulations administered by specialized new bureaucracies. Rather, the rights were stated in broad, relatively simple terms, and precise interpretation was then left to the courts. In other words, the civil justice system was assigned to allocating certain public services by determining the exact degree of entitlement that could legally be exercised by the beneficiaries named in such statutes. Since these entitlements took precedence over the claims of all other service recipients on the pools of public resources provided to finance these services, these interpretations could substantially influence the overall pattern of allocation of each service for which the entitlements involved a significant proportion of the total resource pool.

In a few cases, the entitlement principle was extended even further. These more far-reaching laws did not simply establish eligibility criteria for access to a standardized public service or stipend, they entitled those who met the eligibility standards to individualized services tailored to their own personal needs. Again, how far public service agencies were required to go in providing such tailored responses was left to the courts to determine through the litigative process. In some instances, moreover, the statute provided for ways to make it easier and less expensive for the beneficiaries to initiate litigation to vindicate their rights than would be the case for the ordinary litigant.

What has been the result of federal enactment of such statutes?

Have the courts been flooded with a new and unfamiliar type of lawsuit? Do public agencies find themselves hamstrung by the fact or the fear of litigation? Are public funds being systematically diverted from support of general services to support of those designed for special types of recipients? Or are the diversions from one special service to another? Is the civil justice system an effective forum for reaching decisions about service allocation? Can this approach eventually replace the more traditional dependence on detailed regulations interpreting such statutes?

In addressing such questions, the authors of this study concentrate upon the aftermath of the federal statute that arguably represents the high-water mark of the concept of service allocation by court action: the Education for All Handicapped Children Act of 1975. This statute combines entitlement to individualized service with interpretation by litigation, while also making it relatively easy and cheap for those dissatisfied with government policy to initiate adjudicative action that can readily be appealed to the courts. Moreover, the Act exemplifies another issue raised by the technique in that it represents a federal statutory entitlement that must, as a practical matter, be fulfilled and financed by the state and local authorities that operate the public schools. It also provides an interesting point of comparison with statutes designed to protect and promote the entitlements of such other specialized groups as women, language minority children, the elderly, and handicapped adults.

For all of these reasons the Handicapped Children Act offers a unique analytic prism for examination of the effects of using the civil justice system to determine the distribution of public services among competing claimants. Since this is one of the important frontiers in the evolution of the system, as well as one of the least well-documented, the Institute for Civil Justice has conducted this review of the experience of eight school districts of various sizes and descriptions. Whether the reader's interest is in the capacities of the courts to address such matters, or in the specific effects on educational policy when they do, we believe that the results will be of practical and enduring interest.

Gustave H. Shubert
Director, The Institute for Civil Justice

Executive Summary

This report analyzes the use of the civil justice system to decide the allocation of public services. Its goal is to determine the effects of a trend evident in recent federal legislation—that of giving individuals legally enforceable entitlements to public services. This trend, found in its purest form in the 1975 Education for All Handicapped Children Act (EHA), could radically change the provision of public services.

The new law, PL 94-142, guarantees that every handicapped child will receive, as a matter of right, a "free appropriate public education." Based on the assumption that each handicapped child is unique, the law requires school officials to provide instruction that is tailored specifically to the child's needs.

If the plan proposed for a child's instruction is not appropriate, parents can seek changes under PL 94-142 through a formal due process hearing or in court. Hearing officers and judges can order any changes in the instructional plan, regardless of cost, necessary to make it appropriate to the child's needs. Because some handicapped children require expensive residential placements, the incentives for disputes and costs of settlements may be high.

The provisions of PL 94-142 may have important implications for the courts, school officials, and students. Over 4 million individual plans for the instruction of handicapped students must be negotiated each year; courts would be heavily burdened if only 1 percent of these plans required litigation. School officials must design instructional programs according to strict procedural rules; they must document their judgments to withstand legal scrutiny. Handicapped children and their parents gain important new sources of leverage and may obtain an increasing share of school resources. Nonhandicapped children, lacking a legally enforceable claim to appropriate education, may lose out in the competition for scarce resources.

To assess the consequences of using civil justice procedures to allocate instructional services, we asked the following questions:

1. What are the consequences for the legal system—for the courts in terms of case loads, for judges in terms of complex new issues, and for lawyers in terms of their practice?
2. What are the consequences for local public service agencies, particularly school systems—in terms of their basic ways of doing business and the ability of their professional staffs to use their expertise?
3. What are the consequences for beneficiaries—for those whose rights are protected by the new laws and for those not so protected?

Answers to these questions required a close examination of local responses to the new laws. To obtain the necessary evidence, between November 1980 and August 1981 we conducted extensive interviews in eight school districts in six states. Our sample was small and not statistically representative of the country as a whole, but it included districts in which the effects of the new laws were most likely to be apparent. The sample was designed to enable us to document the effects of civil justice proceedings on school districts where such proceedings have occurred.

The study answered the three research questions on the effects of using civil justice procedures to allocate educational services as follows:

1. The effects on courts are slight.

Few judges had heard cases brought under PL 94-142, and those who had heard cases found them neither difficult nor time-consuming. The vast majority of the disputes about special education services are resolved informally or in the administrative due process system.

2. The effects on school systems are real but limited.

Because school superintendents and board members dread having their actions reviewed in court, most school systems have established administrative units that specialize in administering PL 94-142. These special education staffs bear the burden of coping with the demands of the civil justice system: The school system administrators expect them to settle disputes with parents quickly and to keep the school system from being embarrassed by legally or educationally unsound decisions. Thus, they are less free than other educators to exercise independent professional judgment. They pay the price for protecting the time and working styles of all other district officials.

3. The effects on handicapped children are positive; some benefit more than others.

The positive effects of PL 94-142 are of three kinds. First, state and local funding for education for handicapped children has grown markedly, in part as a result of local officials' eagerness to avoid litigation.

Second, "expensive" services (special placements for handicapped children who cannot be adequately served in district facilities) are available to parents who threaten litigation. Though school districts will not accede to all requests for expensive services, they readily grant those that are well founded in the law; parents also have at least an even chance to prevail if disputes are resolved through the administrative due process system or in court.

Third, handicapped children who do not require expensive services often pay indirectly for the benefits won by litigants, as a result of reductions in the funds available for district-provided special education services. These losses are partly offset by the overall increases in funding for special education. But, parents who have the strongest incentives to litigate can cause transfers of resources from other handicapped children to their own children.

Our most important finding cuts across the three research questions:

- The introduction of civil justice procedures has had an enormous effect on local school policy, despite the low volume of litigation.

The few decisions made by courts affect local policy by establishing a framework for bargaining between school officials and the parents of handicapped children. School officials and parent groups keep close track of legal developments, even developments in courts that are geographically remote and have no local jurisdiction. Though school officials do not automatically implement court orders issued elsewhere, they are reluctant to deny a request for services that is based on any judge's interpretation of the law.

Parents are likewise unlikely to request—and school officials are virtually certain not to grant—a service based on a legal argument that a judge has rejected. In short, courts affect school policy in two ways: first, through their actions, by occasionally issuing decisions that clarify children's entitlements; and second, through their availability, by providing both parents and school officials a sanction (i.e., litigation) that they can use to deter each other from intransigent or unfair bargaining.

We drew two conclusions regarding the use of the civil justice system to decide the allocation of public services:

1. Thanks to the introduction of civil justice methods, PL 94-142 is applied with far more rigorous attention to the rights

and duties of school personnel and beneficiaries than are other federal education programs. It is also run with a smaller regulatory apparatus and with less direct contact between federal officials and local educators than other federal programs of comparable size.
2. Despite these optimistic conclusions, our findings do not necessarily warrant the extension of civil justice procedures to other areas of local educational policy.

The issues that arise in the education of the handicapped are particularly well suited to resolution through judicial process. Several characteristics of special education make it especially amenable to management through civil justice methods, including a premise of individualized entitlements; relatively small numbers of potential disputants; strong incentives for beneficiaries to complain about inequitable treatment; and efficient methods for characterizing disputes and remedies. Few, if any, other areas of local education policy share these characteristics.

The creation of legally enforceable entitlements for students other than the handicapped, or the extension of some general right to "appropriate services" to all children, might have serious consequences. If all students were able to establish their service entitlements through legal process, the allocation of local education budgets would be based on a large number of independent legal actions. Since local budgets are not infinitely flexible, each case settlement would reduce funds available for all other students. All students in a district would be affected but not represented in disputes between individual parents and the school system.

Under these circumstances, the courts would ultimately be forced to make political decisions, establishing multilateral trade-offs among claimants. Though courts can certainly make such decisions, there is no reason or need for them to replace the political processes through which school districts now govern themselves.

Acknowledgments

We want to express our thanks to the numerous respondents in local school and court districts across the country for their cooperation in our research. Without their help, this report would not have been possible.

The data concerning school district decisionmaking were developed in a Rand study supported by the National Institute of Education. We are particularly indebted to Grace Mastalli of NIE for helpful criticism and suggestions.

We also appreciate the assistance of Rand colleagues Richard Shavelson and Lorraine McDonnell, who served as technical reviewers, and Ellen Marks, who provided both data and ideas. Thanks also to Erma Packman for her skillful and timely editing, and to Lee Meyer for her excellent secretarial services.

Contents

FOREWORD iii
EXECUTIVE SUMMARY v
ACKNOWLEDGMENTS ix

Section
I. A NEW ROLE FOR THE CIVIL JUSTICE
   SYSTEM: THE INTERPRETATION OF FEDERAL
   ENTITLEMENT LAWS 1
   Overview of Recent Entitlement Legislation 1
   The Education for All Handicapped Children Act 2
   Questions for Research 6
   Research Methods 7

II. EFFECTS OF THE EDUCATION FOR HANDICAPPED
    CHILDREN ACT 9
    Overview of Findings 9
    Effects on the Legal System 12
    Effects on Local Education Agencies 16
    Effects on Beneficiaries 21

III. CONCLUSIONS 27
     Answers to Research Questions 27
     Suitability of Special Education for Management by
        Civil Justice Methods 29
     Unsuitability of Extending Civil Justice Methods to
        the Management of Other Education Services 31

REFERENCES 33

I. A NEW ROLE FOR THE CIVIL JUSTICE SYSTEM: THE INTERPRETATION OF FEDERAL ENTITLEMENT LAWS

OVERVIEW OF RECENT ENTITLEMENT LEGISLATION

This report analyzes the use of the civil justice system to decide the allocation of public services. Its goal is to determine the effects of a trend evident in recent federal legislation—that of giving individuals legally enforceable entitlements to public services. This trend, found in its purest form in the 1975 Education for All Handicapped Children Act (EHA), could radically change the provision of public services.

Traditionally, public services such as education, police protection, recreation, and public health have been standardized in design and provided to as many users as available funds could cover. Decisions regarding both the design of services and the amount of funds available for them were arrived at through a political process. Executive agencies and legislatures develop designs and funding proposals with a view toward constituents' perceived needs and desires. Debate over alternatives and bargaining to arrive at compromise plans is common.

Some relatively recent federal laws may change the ways that local decisions about education are made. Women, members of minority races or minority language groups, the aged, and the handicapped, specifically, have been guaranteed broad rights of equitable access to public services.[1] Beneficiaries of such laws can seek relief through quasi-judicial processes and ultimately through the courts. Customary local service levels and availability of funds do not limit the benefits that can be ordered.

Most of the service entitlement programs were enacted in the early to mid-1970s, a time of heightened public awareness of historic patterns of discrimination and injustice. Pressures for the reversal of

---

[1] The rights of women are established in Title IX of the Education Amendments of 1972 (PL 92-318). Rights of racial and language minority children are based on Title VI of the Civil Rights Act of 1964, the latter as interpreted by the Supreme Court in the case of *Lau v. Nichols,* 414 U.S. 563 (1974). Rights of the aged are defined in the Age Discrimination Act of 1975, 42 U.S.C. 6101-6107 (1976) as amended by PL 95-478 92 Stat 1555 (1978). For the handicapped, the right of equal access to public services other than education is established by Section 504 of the Rehabilitation Act of 1973, PL 93-112.

those patterns were expressed in terms of rights. The rights were generally formulated in compensatory terms; that is, beneficiaries were guaranteed equal opportunity to benefit from public services, rather than simple access to literally identical services.

Because equal benefits could be defined only in terms of an individual's needs, individual beneficiaries were given a role in determining what services they would receive. The new rights were, in effect, the personal property of individual members of disadvantaged groups, and Congress gave individuals standing to defend their entitlements in court.

At a time when the amount of funds available for new federal domestic activities was dwindling, Congress could not fully subsidize all of the changes in public services required to compensate the holders of newly recognized rights. It could, however, and did establish those rights in statutes and make all federal and federally funded agencies responsible to uphold them.

The new rights guarantees were selective: they created entitlements for only a few groups but did not establish a universal claim to equal public services. In fact, many federal grant programs continued to provide benefits to only a fraction of the eligible beneficiaries. (Examples include Title I of the Elementary and Secondary Education Act [ESEA] and public housing, both of which permit local administrators to concentrate services on a fraction of the eligible population.) Thus, persons covered by one of the new laws had very different service guarantees and more explicit channels for asserting their demands than did most consumers of public services.

By leaving enforcement of rights to the beneficiaries and the courts, Congress eliminated the need for highly detailed rules. Entitlements to services were to be adjudicated on an individual basis, rather than derived from rules written in advance to cover all contingencies. Rules could evolve through judicial interpretation and the use of precedent.

THE EDUCATION FOR ALL HANDICAPPED CHILDREN ACT

Of the entitlememt laws, the Education for All Handicapped Children Act, PL 94-142, has the clearest provisions and most dramatic implications for local policy.[2] It also depends to a greater extent than

---

[2]PL 94-142 89 Stat 773 (1975) (codified at 20 USC 1401-1461 (1976)). For a concise account of the statutory framework see "Enforcing the Right to an 'Appropriate' Education: The Education for All Handicapped Children Act of 1975," *Harvard Law Review*, 92:1103, 1979.

the others on the civil justice system for interpretation and implementation. For these reasons, it is the focus of this study.

Provisions

The first of the two major substantive provisions of PL 94-142 guarantees every handicapped child a "free, appropriate, public education," that is, an education at public expense that takes full account of the individual child's needs and abilities.[3] Handicapped children must receive services appropriate for their individual needs, whether or not those services are customarily offered by the school system. The school system must also pay for auxiliary services that a handicapped child must have in order to benefit from education. These services can include special tutors, therapists, medical treatment, and residential care.

The second major substantive provision of the act guarantees that handicapped children will be educated in the "least restrictive environment" possible, i.e., they will be educated in settings other than regular schools and classrooms only if the required educational services cannot be provided there. These two provisions reflect Congress's understanding of the main dangers facing handicapped children: that local officials might either ignore their needs so as to save money or isolate them in special settings so as to simplify the work of regular classroom teachers.

Although teachers and principals are responsible for identifying handicapped children and planning for their needs, parents also have a central role in the placement process. Parents are presumed to know their handicapped child's needs and abilities better than anyone else, and their views are supposed to count heavily.

At the beginning of each school year, school officials must meet with parents to discuss each handicapped child's individualized educational plan (IEP). That plan must give the parents a written diagnosis of the child's problems, a detailed account of the services that the child will receive, and a statement of the academic objectives that the child is expected to attain during the year. Parents may take exception to any part of the IEP and propose alternatives.

---

[3]The full meaning of this guarantee continues to undergo judicial interpretation and refinement. As the *Rowley* case (*Board of Education of the Hendrick Hudson Central School District, Westchester County et al., v. Amy Rowley*, 50 USLW 4925, June 28, 1982) makes clear, "appropriate" services need not necessarily be "optimal" ones. It is not clear, however, whether the schools may assign a student to one set of services, however good, when another set of services that could be provided are demonstrably better. When there is no professional consensus about what services are best for a student, schools may provide the less costly alternative. But they may not withhold a service known to be more effective.

If the parents and school officials cannot resolve their disagreements informally, questions about the child's IEP are to be resolved in an impartial hearing, conducted under strict due process rules. Either party can appeal the hearing examiner's decision to the state board of education and ultimately to any court of general jurisdiction. A hearing examiner or judge who finds in the parents' favor can order a change in the official description of the child's handicap, the educational services he receives, or both. A proposed educational program can ultimately be judged on only one criterion—its appropriateness to the individual child's needs. Costs are not to be considered.

The rights of children who are not handicapped are less well defined than the rights of handicapped children. Nonhandicapped children, for example, have the right to attend a public school, and some state constitutions require public schools to be of high quality or to provide "thorough and efficient education." But there is no guarantee that public schools will meet each student's individual needs. Parents who are dissatisfied with their children's schooling may demand changes, but school authorities are free to balance those pressures against other requirements, such as expenditure limitations or competing demands from other parents.

The forum in which nonhandicapped children's demands are heard —an informal conference with teachers, an administrative grievance procedure, or a school board meeting—is managed by the school system. The ultimate recourse against an unacceptable decision is political action to change the composition or opinions of the local school board. Parents of handicapped children, in contrast, may turn for ultimate recourse against an unacceptable decision to the civil justice system.

Assumptions and Procedures

The differences in treatment required for handicapped and nonhandicapped children are captured by the administrative law distinction between rulemaking and adjudication.[4] Services for nonhandicapped children are designed and allocated under general rules which managers devise and interpret. Services for handicapped children are designed and allocated through adjudication. In the case of PL 94-142, the process of adjudication has the following features:

- Each handicapped child has a right to appropriate services.

---

[4]See, for example, Gellhorn, Byse, and Strauss (1977, Ch. III).

- Such rights to services are not modified by limits of local resources.
- Beneficiaries (or their parents) may formulate issues in controversy between themselves and school officials and may compel officials to respond to all issues.
- Clear standard procedures must be established for resolving disputes between parents and school officials.
- Hearing examiners and judges have the authority to order changes in the educational services provided to a child.

These "assumptions and procedures of the civil justice system"—as we will refer to the above features of PL 94-142 in the remainder of this report—may have profound effects on the operation of school systems and the distribution of benefits among students. They may also draw the courts into complicated new issues that may compete for places on already overcrowded judicial dockets.[5] PL 94-142 covers 10 percent of all elementary and secondary school students. If disputes about the education of only 1 percent of the nation's handicapped children were resolved in court, the civil justice system could be burdened with over 40,000 new cases per year.

Criticisms

Critics of PL 94-142 charge that its student placement procedures have had several adverse effects on the schools. School superintendents interviewed for several of our previous studies echoed Wise's (1979) conclusion that administrators' time and attention are diverted from substantive educational questions by the need to observe strict procedures.

Some administrators claim that disputes over student placement take up all their time and that they are afraid to make routine educational decisions without legal advice. Superintendents and school board members also note that education for the handicapped has received a rapidly increasing share of their budgets. They claim that the

---

[5]The extension of civil justice procedures into new areas of public life did not begin with these laws. Glazer (1975) commented on the "imperial judiciary" before PL 94-142 became law. Horowitz (1977) focused on education in his study of social policy litigation but considered other classes of social services as well. The concern for possibly adverse effects on public service agencies and courts is also far broader than these laws. Cavanagh and Sarat (1980), for example, evaluated several charges regarding the limits of judicial competence in social policy areas. Wise (1979) presented several of these charges in his book on the "hyper-rationalization" of schooling. He concluded (Chapter 4) that the extension of due process into new areas of school policy had reduced professional discretion, forced teachers to focus on procedural rather than on substantive issues in dealing with students, and produced educationally inappropriate decisions.

threat and reality of legal action is forcing major reallocations of funds away from regular "core" instructional programs.

Because many of the unfavorable accounts of the effects of the new laws come from school administrators advocating a relaxation of federal guarantees, some skepticism seems appropriate. Recent Rand research on education and other public services, however, lends some support to local administrators' complaints. Walker et al. (1980) found that federally mandated services were provided by state and local correction agencies even when other services were being cut for lack of funds. Kimbrough and Hill (1981) noted that the administrative and financial burdens of PL 94-142 were forcing reductions in the services delivered to at least some nonhandicapped students.

The introduction of civil justice assumptions and procedures nevertheless may benefit school officials and nonhandicapped students as well as the handicapped. Disadvantaged groups may be able to use the leverage provided by their access to the courts to increase the total funding available for education. Consistent with the theory of administrative law, adjudication could relieve federal officials of the burden of writing detailed regulations and local officials of the burden of following such regulations.

The loads borne by the courts in creating these benefits may in fact prove to be light. The principal role of the courts as guarantors of fair negotiations between beneficiaries and public officials may prove to be implicit, and they may handle only novel cases or issues that have been mishandled in informal negotiations.

QUESTIONS FOR RESEARCH

Rand's interest in the civil justice system led us to ask whether new laws like PL 94-142 were likely to burden the courts and force judges to handle issues that were unfamiliar, ephemeral, and difficult to resolve. Rand's interest in public policy led us to ask whether such new laws were likely to enhance or interfere with the efficient and equitable delivery of educational services.

Our research focused on the following simple descriptive questions about the consequences of allocating one public service, special education, through the civil justice system:

1. What are the consequences for the legal system—for the courts in terms of case loads and for judges and lawyers in terms of complex new issues?
2. What are the consequences for local school systems—in terms of their ways of doing business, their professionals'

ability to use their expertise, and their administrators' ability to focus their energies on managing services rather than participating in due process hearings or litigation?
3. What are the consequences for service consumers—for handicapped children whose rights are established by PL 94-142 and for students who are not so protected?

RESEARCH METHODS

To answer these questions, we examined the effects of PL 94-142 on courts, public service agencies, and beneficiaries. But, we hoped to generalize beyond one program to determine the likely effects of widespread use of public service entitlements. To do this, we had to go beyond the simple description of the effects of PL 94-142, to explain the processes by which those effects came about, and to distinguish those processes that are clearly unique to PL 94-142 from those that would be general to any program based on individual entitlements to public services.

For purposes of comparison, we examined local responses to the following laws that protect the rights of various groups to equal access to public services: Title IX of the Education Amendments of 1972 (women); Title VI of the Civil Rights Act of 1964 (language minority children); the Age Discrimination Act of 1975 (the elderly); Section 504 of the Rehabilitation Act of 1973 (handicapped adults).

To obtain the necessary evidence, between November 1980 and August 1981 we conducted case studies in eight school districts in six states. Our school districts varied in size from the very small (less than 5000 students) to the very large (over 500,000 students), and represented urban, suburban, and rural areas. Three districts were in states whose courts had been involved deeply in educational issues before the enactment of PL 94-142. All of the districts were near metropolitan areas that, according to officials of the Office of Education for the Handicapped, U.S. Department of Education, had well-developed public interest organizations working on behalf of the handicapped, women, and language minority groups.

Our sample was small and it represented districts in which the effects of the new laws were most likely to be apparent. It was designed to enable us to document the effects of civil justice proceedings on school districts. However, our sample is not statistically representative of the country as a whole. Though our findings are likely to exaggerate the frequency with which beneficiaries use the courts and quasi-judicial processes, they accurately represent the consequences of those proceedings when they occur.

We spent from two to five days in each school district, interviewing:

- The school district's director of special education and other special education staff members who had been involved in litigation and administrative hearings
- One or more top school district officials—in most cases, the school superintendent or deputy superintendent
- Officers or staff members of special education advocacy groups
- Parents (identified by school officials and advocacy groups) who had initiated or threatened legal action under PL 94-142
- Attorneys who advised or represented the parents whom we interviewed, or were generally active on behalf of handicapped children
- Judges who had heard PL 94-142 cases. (In the cases of judges who refused to be interviewed, we interviewed their law clerks.)

In these interviews, we gathered information to build case files on the following topics:

- The history and resolution of local quasi-judicial proceedings and litigation conducted under one or another of the new federal laws
- The effects of such proceedings on school district decision-making processes
- The consequences of case settlements for other recipients of public education.

The authors conducted all interviews; both interviewed respondents whenever possible. When joint interviewing was impossible, we ensured reliability by reviewing results and our interpretations of them soon after meeting with a respondent, and, if necessary, we rechecked facts and interpretations by telephone.

II. EFFECTS OF THE EDUCATION FOR HANDICAPPED CHILDREN ACT

OVERVIEW OF FINDINGS

In this section, we present our findings about the effects of federal service entitlement laws, and specifically, the Education for All Handicapped Children Act, on the legal system, school systems, and beneficiaries. Our most important findings may be summarized as follows:

- Litigation under federal service entitlement laws is rare.
- Civil justice proceedings under PL 94-142 powerfully affect local educational policy and services, and cases do not have to be decided locally to be influential.
- PL 94-142 successfully demonstrates that civil justice procedures can substitute for the detailed regulations and complex enforcement apparatus typical of federal education programs.

Litigation Under Federal Entitlement Laws

Only five of the eight school districts that we visited had been party to civil actions concerning the rights of women or language minority groups. The few cases brought under those guarantees concerned employment—the hiring and promotion of teachers and support staff—rather than services to children. Pressure to improve services for girls or language minority groups was applied through the normal administrative and political channels, not through the courts. The same was true for action on behalf of the handicapped under Section 504.

The Education for All Handicapped Children Act was the only significant source of legal action on the local level.[1] At least one complete administrative due process hearing had been held in each district that we visited; larger districts reported as many as 20 during the past five years. Many districts had had one, and some had several, disputes resolved in court.

The fact that litigation focused on only one law was initially surprising, given the level of alarm previously expressed by school officials and the potential leverage that beneficiaries could gain by going to court. On closer examination, however, the reasons for the predomi-

---

[1] Plaintiffs' briefs in such cases also frequently cited Section 504 of the Rehabilitation Act. The main legal arguments in those cases, however, were always formulated in terms of PL 94-142.

nance of PL 94-142 as a source of legal action became clear. This law encourages legal action by keeping plaintiffs' costs of initiating legal action low and by permitting successful plaintiffs, particularly parents, to obtain financially valuable settlements. None of the other mandates that we studied has these features.

PL 94-142 keeps plaintiffs' entry costs low by starting the legal process with the administrative due process hearing. Once requested, hearings must be held within 30 days and at public expense. Parents need not have legal representation, but counsel is often available free from public interest groups or advocacy law firms funded by foundations or the federal government.

Parents may obtain all of the school district records on their child's educational evaluation and placement, and the school system must pay for any additional testing or expert witnesses required by the hearing examiner. This process lets parents assemble their cases quickly and at low cost. It also sharpens the points at issue and completes the discovery process, so that the groundwork is laid for any appeals to higher administrative bodies or to courts.

Settlements

The monetary value of settlements under PL 94-142 may be considerable. Special education services are costly; even relatively minor services, such as tutoring, may cost hundreds of dollars per year. Many parents paid for such services themselves before the enactment of PL 94-142. More heroic services, such as psychotherapy, training in specialized schools, or placement in full-time residential facilities, can cost tens of thousands of dollars per year.

For the parents of an autistic child who may require residential placements throughout his elementary and secondary school years, the full value of an award—even net contributions from health insurance—may be well over $100,000. Although few parents could have paid for these services in any case, legal action under PL 94-142 may help them to avoid either paying for costly day care or other custodial arrangements, or placing the child in a public institution.

The other mandates that we set out to study impose far higher costs on plaintiffs and offer outcomes that are either largely symbolic or of indeterminate financial value. Under these statutes plaintiffs must pay for both their own legal counsel and the discovery process. Courts can award legal fees to prevailing plaintiffs, but the costs of unsuccessful litigation may be high and potential awards limited.

Under Title IX, for example, parents may win their daughter's entry into a vocational education class previously open only to boys, or open up previously closed athletic or physical education programs.[2] These may be valuable outcomes, but they do not save the parents money, or obtain costly services that the family cannot afford. Given the nature of benefits available under mandates other than PL 94-142, parents in the districts that we studied made their demands through political channels or informal conferences with school officials and left legal action to national interest groups pursuing class actions.

Consistent with these findings, most of the detailed results that we report below apply only to the local effects of PL 94-142. Other laws have produced no results to report here.

Influence of Civil Justice Procedures on Local Education Policy and Services

Local school officials monitor the development of PL 94-142 legal precedents and implement new court orders even when the orders are issued by courts that have no local jurisdiction. This process of voluntary local implementation is encouraged by the U.S. Department of Education, which disseminates the results of PL 94-142 litigation to superintendents, special education professionals, and local handicapped parents' groups.[3] The distaste of school officials for direct involvement in litigation (discussed in detail below) motivates the voluntary response.

Local school officials anticipate local parents' demand for services that have been ordered by courts elsewhere and handle the vast majority of requests in routine administrative channels. Those few local issues that end in court are highly personalized, often unique. School systems resist parent demands only when the services requested are expensive or unusual and the local district's obligation to provide them is not clearly established by statute or precedent. On rare occasions, litigation on such issues can lead to landmark legal decrees. In the districts that we studied, most issues resolved through litigation were idiosyncratic and had no broader significance.

Civil Justice Procedures as a Substitute for Regulations and Enforcement

PL 94-142 has far less elaborate regulations and requires a far smaller federal administrative effort than other major national

---

[2]On the kinds of changes gained by complainants under Title IX, see Hill and Rettig (1980).

[3]For a general description of U.S. Department of Education's role in the operation of PL 94-142, see Hill and Marks (1982).

categorical programs and civil rights guarantees.[4] The availability of courts to resolve disputes eliminates the need for exhaustive regulations. Parents' interest in obtaining benefits for their handicapped children ensures that new legal precedents will be widely disseminated and applied, and school officials' fear of being embarrassed in court guarantees that most educators will become informed about their legal obligations and try assiduously to stay in compliance.

The following three themes underlie the detailed discussion of the ways in which PL 94-142 has affected courts, school systems, and beneficiaries:

- PL 94-142 may be a unique case.
- The broad application of civil justice assumptions and procedures to education policymaking may not be warranted.
- The immediate evidence on PL 94-142 is far more benign than we had initially expected.

EFFECTS ON THE LEGAL SYSTEM

The infrequency of local litigation noted above makes our main finding obvious: cases connected with PL 94-142 did not burden any court. Few judges heard more than one case concerning a handicapped child's placement, and most heard none. Although cases may be filed in municipal and state courts, plaintiffs' lawyers usually prefer to use federal courts on the assumption that federal judges are more likely to be familiar with the relevant law and precedents. Nevertheless, even though PL 94-142 litigation has been concentrated in the federal courts, it represents an insignificant part of most federal dockets.

Courts and Judges

We interviewed several current and retired federal district court judges about the PL 94-142 cases that they had heard. None considered the cases particularly complex or difficult to resolve. In fact, PL 94-142 neither challenged the courts' competence nor competed for their time.

---

[4]For a comparison of the federal government's administrative arrangements under PL 94-142 and other federal education programs, see Hill and Marks (1982).

Some of the judges had heard suits brought against state institutions for the handicapped under Section 504 of the Rehabilitation Act of 1973. Many such cases were time consuming because the judges had to delve in detail into the institutional treatment of severely handicapped individuals. Judges in those cases usually retained jurisdiction to monitor the implementation of ordered reforms in state institutions. The monitoring process typically required a few days of court time per year for several years. None of the judges regarded even those cases as significant burdens on their time or skills.

Some interviewed judges expressed the fear that the right to litigate over public services might enable beneficiaries and service providers to collude against local school boards and state legislatures. Some believed that early lawsuits on the education of the handicapped had been engineered by interest groups and service providers to obtain by judicial decree funds that could not be won in open political contests.

As examples, our respondents cited the *PARC*[5] and *Mills*[6] cases, which predated PL 94-142. In both cases, parents of handicapped children sued state education officials to obtain improved instructional programs. School officials conceded that plaintiffs' children were entitled to the services requested, but claimed that appropriations were inadequate. The parties entered consent decrees that greatly expanded handicapped children's rights to services. State and local officials, obligated thereby to find funds for those services, faced contempt citations if they failed. Rather than force these officials to face judicial punishment, the legislatures and school boards in the affected areas provided the necessary funds. Thus, our respondents believed, handicapped parents and allied school personnel were able to use the court's authority to obtain appropriations that legislative bodies had previously not provided.

Administrative Due Process

Whether or not the judges' concerns regarding collusion were well founded, we saw little evidence of it between plaintiffs and defendants in local PL 94-142 disputes. Disputes that go to administrative due process hearings or to court are real. Parents who brought complaints believed that school officials had offered less than their children

---

[5]*Pennsylvania Association for Retarded Children v. Pennsylvania*, 343 F. Supp 279, 307 (E.D. Pa. 1972).
[6]*Mills v. Board of Education*, 348 F. Supp 866, 880 (D.D.C. 1972). Both cases are discussed in detail in Kirp, Buss, and Kuriloff (1974).

needed; on their part, school officials were frequently offended by parents' challenges to their professional judgment. A few cases are amicable—for example, cases in which school officials do not oppose the parents' novel request but are reluctant to grant it without the added sanction of a judge's or hearing examiner's order. Our fieldwork uncovered no evidence that parents and school officials had contrived a dispute to increase their joint leverage on funding sources. Local special education staffs and parents of the handicapped are often political allies, but their alliance is frequently strained by disagreements over proper treatment for individual students.

The infrequency of judicial involvement in PL 94-142 does not accurately indicate the number of legal issues that arise in the program's operation. Based on case disposition data obtained from four state education agencies, we estimate that fewer than one in ten disputes handled by the administrative due process system is ever appealed to a court.

The administrative due process system offers plaintiffs the same kinds of protections and results as the courts, but at greater speed and lower cost. Parents and school officials are therefore generally eager to settle their disputes informally or in the administrative due process system. Because both parties can threaten to raise the cost of a dispute by appealing it to the courts, both have the incentive to bargain seriously in the administrative due process system. As many of our respondents commented, the availability of the system also gives school officials a powerful incentive to maintain procedures that look fair and competent.

By handling disputes in which the stakes are extremely high or relations between the disputants have become acrimonious, the courts also serve as a safety valve for the administrative due process system. School officials whom we interviewed reported that they had occasionally refused to accept a hearing examiner's order to provide an extremely expensive or unusual service and had sought resolution of the case in court. On other occasions disputes over relatively minor issues led to such intense personal animosity between parents and school officials that resolution was impossible in any forum operated by the school system.

Advocacy Lawyers

In the districts that we studied, the part of the local legal system most affected by PL 94-142 was the public interest bar. At that time, public advocacy law firms existed in or near most of our sample school districts. Some were staffed by part-time volunteer practitioners, but most were funded by foundation grants, interest group treasuries, or federal programs. Some represented a variety of disadvantaged clients, but the ones generally regarded as most influential specialized in the rights of the handicapped. Most such firms had close working relationships with local associations of the parents of handicapped children.

The basis for most advocacy attorneys' influence was successful representation of handicapped clients. Most had brought their first cases in the mid-1970s and built reputations as the first plaintiffs' lawyers to win changes in educational policy. The reputations of others, predating PL 94-142, were based on successful suits brought under state constitutional guarantees.

The winning of one important case was sufficient to give an advocacy attorney access to top school officials and enormous bargaining leverage. In most of the districts we visited, the advocacy attorneys were generally recognized as the local persons who were best informed about parents' and children's rights.

School officials therefore hesitated to deny attorneys' requests on behalf of children and to let a dispute with the attorney end in court. In a few of our sample districts, school officials had adopted advocacy attorneys as their de facto legal advisers. In one district, school officials routinely consulted the most prominent advocacy attorney about how to handle cases brought by other plaintiffs' lawyers. The school system avoided conflict with an advocate by granting the services that he requested on behalf of clients and by voluntarily implementing the results of cases that he had won in other districts. For his part, the attorney tried to give balanced advice when asked about cases brought by other attorneys, so that school officials were comfortable in either granting or opposing those requests.

Most advocacy attorneys practiced in several school districts and worked to build statewide reputations. In two states, individual advocacy attorneys had gained virtual veto power over state regulations and statutes: local school officials were so eager to avoid tangling with the advocates that they pressed state government officials to head off litigation by clearing new policies in advance.

Advocacy law on behalf of the handicapped is not lucrative, and most of the prominent plaintiffs' attorneys either earned low salaries or treated their advocacy work as a *pro bono* sideline. This work paid off enormously, however, in terms of political influence. As one such attorney said in an interview, "This is far better than running for the school board or the state legislature. People call to ask my opinion. I didn't have to run for office or sit through meetings about things that don't interest me."

A few advocates have succeeded in extending their influence into other policy areas. Their reputation as effective litigators gave them considerable leverage in a variety of civil rights areas. One attorney parlayed a reputation gained in handicapped litigation into opportunities to represent clients in nationally publicized First Amendment cases. Most, however, have their greatest degree of influence in dealing with special education policy.

In general, the part of the civil justice system concerned with the rights of the handicapped involves a minuscule part of the local legal community. The law of the handicapped does, however, provide an opportunity for a small number of attorneys to develop an influential, if not lucrative, practice.

EFFECTS ON LOCAL EDUCATION AGENCIES

We chose our sample districts because they had been involved in legal actions under PL 94-142. The volume of legal activity in our sample districts, although not great, was higher than average. Kirst and Bertken's 1980 survey of administrative due process claims in California and our own questions to state education agency officials show that only a few school districts have any appreciable level of litigation or administrative due process disputes.

Only a small proportion, certainly less than 10 percent, of the nation's 17,000 school districts has ever been party to a PL 94-142 court case. A few dozen school districts, concentrated in and around the nation's largest metropolitan areas, have been to court more than five times under PL 94-142. Most school districts have handled at least one administrative due process complaint, and the largest metropolitan districts handle ten or more each year. Only the smallest rural districts have completely avoided formal disputes. Those districts, though numerous, serve only a small fraction of the nation's elementary and secondary school districts.

Our case studies enable us to report on the effects of PL 94-142 litigation on school districts that have been to court and have conducted more than one or two administrative hearings. In interpreting our findings, the reader must remember that our sample districts were involved in PL 94-142 legal actions to an unusually high degree.

Top Officials

Our case studies examined the effects of legal action on top school district officials, particularly school superintendents and board members. In the course of conducting earlier studies on the effects of federal education programs, we had been told that school officials' time was dominated by PL 94-142 legal actions, that they were constantly in court or negotiating with parents under threat of litigation, and that they were unable to make any important policy decisions without seeking legal advice.

Had we conducted our fieldwork in the first or second years of PL 94-142's existence, rather than six years later, we might have found that school officials were inundated by actions resulting from PL 94-142. Local school officials told us that they saw their first legal disputes as major crises. School superintendents themselves undertook negotiations with complaining parents, and any decision to contest parents' claims in court was reviewed by the school board. In those instances, top officials spent major portions of their time negotiating, consulting with attorneys, and attending hearings.

By 1981, however, top officials in most of our sample districts were spending little or no time on PL 94-142 legal actions or negotiations and rarely seeking legal advice. They are now usually well insulated from legal actions and from day-to-day negotiations with the parents of handicapped children. School board members consider special education when they make the annual budget, and the superintendent maintains normal managerial control over subordinates who run special education programs. Board members and superintendents usually know that the parents of handicapped children are well organized and well informed and that they have ready access to the courts; they therefore attend to special education budget requests and other demands made by local special education advocates. But, top officials deal with special education in the course of their normal political and managerial transactions, not as a unique concern dominated by legal issues.

Special Education Staffs

School systems learned quickly to protect top officials by routinizing and bureaucratizing the response to legal issues. After their first encounters with the PL 94-142 legal process, most school systems strengthened their special education divisions by hiring or training experts in the PL 94-142 student placement process. These units were established in the district's central office, usually two or three levels below the superintendent.[7]

The school systems also obtained competent legal advice, either by

---

[7]This process of creating a specialized bureaucracy in response to a new external threat is well documented. See, for example, Hill and Marks (1982) and Meyer (1979).

adding qualified lawyers to the special education staff or by retaining competent private counsel. These attorneys were available to advise the board and superintendent, but their real job was to assist the mid-level employees responsible for the day-to-day operation of the district's special education program.

The student placement process for special education is complex and time consuming, but it imposes the greatest demands on the specialists who were expressly hired to manage it.[8] District directors of special education were apparently the source of many of the complaints that we heard before we began this study. They are heavily burdened by the PL 94-142 requirement that they prepare and defend individualized education plans for all handicapped students, and they definitely spend less time supervising student instruction now than before PL 94-142 was enacted. Their jobs have changed in these ways because higher officials, e.g., superintendents, insisted on being protected from the legal process.

It is clear from our interviews that school officials at all levels dread being involved in legal processes. Virtually all school officials regard themselves as educators—teachers and curriculum designers—rather than as executors of laws and regulations. For them, litigation (and negotiations conducted under the threat of litigation) are time-consuming distractions from their chosen professional activities.

Legal processes also impose unfamiliar methods of decisionmaking and expose educators to scrutiny under other than their own professional standards. Some believe that the artful and intuitive processes by which teachers assess children's needs cannot be translated into the language of courts and due process hearings. Others fear being embarrassed or abused by opposing lawyers.

Parents' Leverage

Educators' aversion to the legal process provides a potential source of leverage for the parents of handicapped children. Though parents cannot always get everything they think their children need, their access to the legal system predisposes school officials to take their requests seriously. Special education administrators try to keep parents satisfied, and to resolve conflicts quickly and informally, before anyone initiates a complaint or court action. Higher-level officials, also wanting to avoid becoming entangled in legal conflicts, try to find resources to deliver services promised by the special education staff.

---

[8]For an account of the arrangements necessary to implement the PL 94-142 student placement process, see Stearns et al. (1980).

From our interviews it was clear that top officials' eagerness to have issues settled at lower levels is the key to parents' leverage. Special education staff must assume that every dissatisfied parent is a potential complainant. The fact that many parents belong to local advocacy organizations makes the implicit threat of litigation credible. Many such organizations keep one or two complaints in process at all times as a reminder to local officials that the prospect of legal action is real.

School systems cannot, of course, grant every parent's request. Once a school district has committed all of its funds, it has great difficulty granting a request to purchase new services or to staff a new program. Some conflicts with parents are, in addition, simply beyond district officials' control. The experts hired to diagnose handicapped children and prescribe services are often independent professionals (e.g., psychiatrists, clinical psychologists, audiologists, and speech pathologists) who develop their own views about children's needs. When parents and experts disagree, the district can do little to avoid legal action.

School district officials can usually avoid legal action by taking account of parents' opinions and by keeping themselves informed about the relevant laws, regulations, and precedents. District special education staff consider the legally correct handling of the student placement process their most important responsibility. They told us that they were supposed to avoid legal action whenever possible.

When administrative due process hearings or court cases are inevitable, district special education staff believe that their recommendations must be right. A record of adverse judgments on educational or legal grounds can hurt special education officials, first, by earning the disapproval of top district officials and, second, by encouraging parents to doubt the correctness of special education placements and thus to contest them more often.

Attention to Legal Issues

Few student placement decisions involve subtle legal issues. Because the federal government has left the detailed interpretation of PL 94-142 to the courts, however, judicial interpretations and precedents are closely monitored by both parent groups and school administrators.

The most significant issues have been addressed in nationally publicized cases, argued on parents' behalf by nationally prominent advocacy lawyers. Issues clarified in those cases include handicapped children's rights to psychotherapy, catheterization, and year-round schooling.[9] Parents' interest group networks spread the news about landmark decisions and urge local parents to demand similar services. The inclination to avoid unnecessary conflict with activist parents forces local administrators to keep abreast of new legal developments.

In local education agencies, such fine attention to the law is unique to special education. The degree to which local officials have become aware of their legal obligations under PL 94-142 is apparent only in comparison with local response to other federal legal requirements. Local officials responsible for other federal programs allegedly seldom fully understand the meaning of the laws and regulations that they administer.

Studies of ESEA Title I—the federal program that has the most complete code of regulations and pays for the largest number of salaries for the largest number of local administrative specialists—have shown that local officials know a few of the program's basic legal principles, but lack a detailed knowledge of the law and cannot accurately judge whether a particular service arrangement is proper or not.[10] Parent groups for Title I and other programs are far less active and less focused than parents of the handicapped. Few Title I parents know about their children's legal rights and seldom question whether the program is providing the right services to the right students. Local Title I coordinators wait for state or federal officials to inform them of new requirements or identify violations.

Coordinators of other federal programs typically know even less than the officials in charge of Title I. Hill and Rettig (1980) showed that local coordinators for Title IX and Section 504 seldom knew what their own duties were and had no day-to-day responsibilities. They were typically appointed only to establish *pro forma* compliance with regulatory requirements, and their chief tasks were to file assurances of compliance and answer inquiries from state or federal agencies.

The Hill and Rettig study also provides a base for comparing PL 94-142 administrative due process arrangements with other grievance procedures maintained by local school systems. The purely administrative grievance procedures required under Title IX and Section 504 were not run according to strict due process standards, nor were their

---

[9]Regarding rights to psychotherapy see *Lora et al. v. Board of Education of the City of New York*, 456 F. Supp 1211, 1214 (E.D.N.Y. 1978), and *North v. D.C. Board of Education*, EHR 551:557 (D.D.C. 1979). Regarding catheterization see *Tatro v. State of Texas*, 481 F. Supp 1224 (N.D. Texas 1979). Regarding year-round schooling see *Armstrong v. Kline*, 476 F. Supp 583 (E.D. Pa. 1979).

[10]See, for example, National Institute of Education (1977), Silverstein (1977), and Hill (1979).

outcomes reviewable by higher agencies or courts. Those procedures were seldom well organized or unbiased. Grievances were heard by school employees who tried to mollify complainants. Though some complainants were satisfied with the outcome, few left the grievance process with a good understanding of the legal basis on which their cases had been resolved.

Special education administrators are members of a distinct profession, and they are dedicated to the welfare of their clients—handicapped children. Most strongly support the principles of PL 94-142. Given the defensive role assigned them by their superiors in the school district organization, they pay a high price if they fail to perform as the law requires.

The defensive orientation of special education administrators to the law is evident in the way they apply new legal precedents. Those in our sample responded quickly to any parent who based a request for services on a new legal principle, but they did not routinely inform parents about new legal doctrines that might affect their children's placements. Administrators tried to limit extensions of services to those children whose parents were "in the know" about new legal developments.

In summary, the use of the civil justice system in the implementation of PL 94-142 has had important effects on school systems. It has made officials highly responsive to claims advanced by knowledgeable parents, and it has ensured that officials know exactly what their legal obligations are. As the next section will detail, the civil justice features of PL 94-142 have also made district officials highly responsive to parents who know the law and use it aggressively to obtain special benefits for their children.

EFFECTS ON BENEFICIARIES

PL 94-142 has significantly increased the funding available for special education. However, the federal grant program established by PL 94-142 accounts for only a small part of the increase. Since the enactment of PL 94-142, federal funding has grown to more than $1 billion per year, and state and local funding has more than doubled, to over $11 billion. On average, services to handicapped children now cost more than twice as much per capita as services to nonhandicapped children.[11]

---

[11]For a complete analysis of the costs of special education services, see Kakalik et al. (1981).

More and Better Special Educational Services

The growth in funding for handicapped children reflects the same political consensus in favor of improving special education that led to the passage of PL 94-142. It also reflects the leverage that PL 94-142 created for the handicapped by giving beneficiaries access to the courts in order to obtain a "free appropriate public education."

School officials in many of our sample districts report that local funding was increased to head off litigation. School systems mounted programs to identify handicapped children and place them in special education as quickly as possible. "Handicapped" was interpreted broadly, and many children were identified as mildly handicapped and offered services that their parents had not thought of requesting—for example, speech therapy and "adaptive physical education." Campaigns to identify handicapped students succeeded so well that many districts developed long lists of children awaiting placement in special education. Placements required significant new teacher hiring and the creation of special remedial programs in many schools. During the late 1970s, school boards and state legislatures voted larger and larger appropriations for special education, and it became the fastest-growing part of most educational budgets.

As noted in the previous section, handicapped children benefit from the establishment of disciplined professional placement processes. Parents can usually rely on the school districts to conduct good professional assessments of their children's needs and offer the most nearly appropriate services available from local sources. This procedure satisfies the vast majority of parents, who have no fixed ideas about what their children should receive.

A small group of handicapped children and their parents, however, derive extra benefits from the civil justice aspects of PL 94-142—sometimes at the expense of handicapped children whose parents are less assertive. By threatening court action as provided for by PL 94-142, litigious parents are able to obtain for their handicapped children expensive special educational programs not routinely provided by the school system.

Such programs are expensive because they must be purchased from special vendors. They include full-time residential placements, e.g., for autistic or severely disturbed children; placement in private day schools, e.g., for children who require training that no local public school is equipped to provide; and special tutoring, e.g., for deaf or blind students who cannot benefit from the services that the school system routinely offers such students. These services vary in cost from several hundred to many tens of thousands of dollars per year. But since they all require expenditures outside the school system's regular capital and staff budgets, they can impose severe financial burdens.

Only a small minority of handicapped children require such services. Most require only services that the school system is staffed and equipped to deliver, i.e., routine tutoring, counseling, mobility assistance, access to braille instruction, or placement in a classroom whose teacher uses sign language for the deaf.

Since 1975, the larger school districts have developed an enormously varied set of special education resources, frequently including specialized schools for the severely handicapped. The needs that those districts cannot meet from their own resources are rare and specialized. Small rural districts, on the other hand, offer only a limited set of routine services and must buy a higher proportion of special education services from other school districts or from proprietary schools.

School officials whom we interviewed, especially those in the larger and better-equipped districts, admitted forthrightly that they resist purchasing services from outside the school system. It is, therefore, not surprising that most of the legal disputes in our sample districts concerned placements outside district facilities.[12] Typically, parents had identified a specific placement or service that they wanted for their child and would not accept the alternative program offered by the school district.

In some cases that we examined, school officials offered to provide services similar in design to ones that a child had been receiving from a private institution. The child's parents rejected the school's recommendation, insisting on continuing a private placement in which they had confidence. In other cases, the district offered a different service from that requested by the parents, e.g., placement in a district-run day center for autistic children, rather than a full-time residential facility. In all cases, the issue to be decided was whether the school district's proposed education plan was, in the terms established by PL 94-142, "appropriate" to the individual child's needs.

---

[12]A less common but still important type of dispute was initiated by parents who believed that school officials had exaggerated the severity of their child's problems. Some parents categorically rejected the notion that their children were handicapped; others agreed that their children were handicapped, but thought that the district had exaggerated the severity of the child's handicap. In such cases, parents petitioned to remove "stigmatizing" labels from their children's records and to obtain educational placements that were "normal" (i.e., in regular classroom settings) or as "normal" as possible. Since PL 94-142 guarantees that children will be served in "the least restrictive environment," parents are well within their rights to oppose an unnecessarily stigmatizing label or resist an overly restrictive placement. School officials, on their part, are responsible both to make a correct assessment of the child's needs and to avoid burdening regular classroom teachers with problems that can be handled only in a specialized setting. These disputes seldom have major financial implications for the parents or the school system, but they often stir strong emotions and can be difficult to settle without judicial authority.

Eased Financial Burdens for Some Parents

A rich source of data on the issues in due process disputes is provided by Kirst and Bertken (1981). They tabulated the issues and results of all California PL 94-142 administrative due process hearings conducted between 1976 and 1980. Their data show that more than 80 percent of the hearings involved parents' requests for services provided by private vendors rather than by school system employees. In 38 percent of those cases, the child was already being served by the private vendor, at parents' expense. In such cases, the vendor frequently gave the parents technical and procedural advice and occasionally provided legal representation.

According to Kirst and Bertken, relatively few parents use the administrative system and the courts. Based on their data and figures that we obtained from several state and local education agencies, we estimate that fewer than 1 percent of all children served under PL 94-142 ever become the subject of a formal dispute. A disproportionate share of the disputants are high-income, well-educated parents. Such parents are the most likely to have specific ideas about the services their children should receive. The administrative due process system itself, according to Kirst and Bertken, does not favor high-income plaintiffs. Low-income parents, though less likely to use the administrative due process system, are slightly more likely than high-income parents to prevail in the cases that they bring.

The average settlement won by parents is relatively valuable. Kirst and Bertken estimate that on average the private day school tuitions granted in administrative due process hearings cost nearly twice as much as the average per pupil cost of special education. Students granted full-time residential placement received services that cost five times as much as standard special education.

Funding Advantages Over Other Groups

We tried in our fieldwork to learn how the expensive services awarded through legal dispute were paid for. We wanted to know whether such services were funded by increased appropriations, by cuts in services to nonhandicapped students, or by reallocation of resources among handicapped children. We found that the situation had changed since the early days of PL 94-142. During the first few years of the program, appropriations for special education grew enough to provide across-the-board increases in service quality. Handicapped children who required standard special education services (e.g., part-time tutoring or speech therapy) got help more frequently and from better-qualified instructors. School districts also quickly complied with orders to provide expensive residential or private vendor services.

As education funding was reduced by the fiscal limitation movements and recession of the late 1970s, school systems maintained the quality of special education services by diverting funds from other categorical grant programs. Access to the judicial system gave the handicapped an enormous competitive advantage over other interest groups. State and local funding for other disadvantaged groups (e.g., the poor and non-English-speaking minorities) barely held steady while special education grew.

According to Kimbrough and Hill (1981), federal funds intended to support such objectives as school desegregation and compensatory instruction in low-income schools were used to pay for special education, and services to students previously served by the donor programs were cut. That same study also found that increases for special education did not cut into funding for general school district administration and regular classroom instruction. Thus, it appears that PL 94-142 gave the handicapped an advantage over other groups that required special treatment. It did not, however, divert funds from the majority of children for whom the basic "core curriculum" was designed.

New Political Problems

Because of severe cuts in federal and state grants in the early 1980s, few school districts have been able to divert new funds or personnel into special education. Expensive services to individual students must therefore be purchased from a fixed or shrinking special education budget. State education agencies at one time used part of the funds that they received from PL 94-142 to help districts pay for expensive services (Thomas, 1981). However, those funds are now fully committed, and some states, including two in our sample, have had to renege on promises to help districts pay for special residential placements.

State support of special education will likely continue to dwindle (Thomas, 1982). Local budgets once contained contingency funds for unexpectedly large expenditures, but those are now either eliminated or completely committed, especially in districts in large metropolitan areas, where most of the litigation for expensive services takes place. As our respondents explained, expensive services to a few students can now be funded only by reducing the level of special education services provided by district-paid staff. Because of those reductions, handicapped children who receive standard special education services receive them slightly less often or in larger groups. Newly identified handicapped children must stay a few weeks longer on waiting lists before they can be served.

These effects on the distribution of local resources have created political problems for the handicapped. The cohesion of local handicapped advocacy groups is threatened by the fact that expensive services won by a few force reductions in the levels of resources available for the majority of handicapped children. Some factions within local handicapped parents' groups are trying to discourage parents who would use the courts to obtain private vendor services similar to those available from the school system.

In addition, groups representing nonhandicapped students (e.g., parents of low-income, non-English-speaking, and gifted children) are trying to reduce the advantages enjoyed by the handicapped. Some have pressed for reinterpretations of PL 94-142 that would place their children under its protection. Others, e.g., Hispanic groups, have pushed for laws or regulations that would establish similar rights for non-English-speaking children.

We cannot say at this writing whether the level of requests for expensive services under PL 94-142 will increase or decrease. If local parent groups succeed in limiting the number of requests for expensive services, the handicapped can probably continue to enjoy the benefits of special access to the courts. If, however, handicapped advocacy groups continue to fight among themselves and other groups continue to demand similar protection, the benefits described above may be seriously diluted. The final section of this report will consider the likely effects of federal laws that would allow groups other than the handicapped to use legal processes to establish their children's rights to services.

III. CONCLUSIONS

We started this study with questions about the consequences of using the assumptions and procedures of the civil justice system to allocate public services. In particular, we asked how PL 94-142, a law that requires school systems to resolve disputes about special education services through judicially reviewable due process hearings, had affected the local legal community, the local school system, and the intended beneficiaries.

We found that the introduction of civil justice procedures has had an enormous effect on local school policy, despite the low volume of litigation. The few decisions made by courts affect local policy by establishing a framework for bargaining between school officials and the parents of handicapped children.

We found also that school officials and parent groups keep close track of legal developments, even in courts that are geographically remote and have no local jurisdiction. Although school officials do not automatically implement court orders issued elsewhere, they are reluctant to deny a request for services that is based on any judge's interpretation of the law. Parents are likewise unlikely to request—and school officials are virtually certain not to grant—a service based on a legal argument that a judge has rejected.

In short, we found that courts affect school policy in two ways: first, through their actions, by occasionally issuing decisions that clarify children's entitlements; and second, through their availability, by providing both parents and school officials a sanction (i.e., litigation) that they can use to deter each other from intransigent or unfair bargaining.

ANSWERS TO RESEARCH QUESTIONS

We found the following answers to our three specific research questions:

1. The effects on courts are slight.

Few judges heard even one case brought under PL 94-142, and those who heard cases found them neither difficult nor time-consuming. The vast majority of the disputes about special education services are resolved informally or in the administrative due process system. The main role of the courts is to provide parents and school officials with incentives to negotiate fairly with each other; disputants are deterred from bargaining carelessly by the fact that their actions can ultimately be reviewed in court.

2. The effects on school systems are real but limited.

Because school superintendents and board members dread having their actions reviewed in court, most school systems have established administrative units that specialize in administering PL 94-142. These special education staffs bear the burden of coping with the demands of the civil justice system: the school system administrators expect them to settle disputes with parents quickly and to keep the school system from being embarrassed by legally or educationally unsound decisions. Special education administrators, therefore, have a strong incentive to keep informed about their legal obligations and to deal fairly with parents. They dislike working under tight substantive and procedural constraints, and they are less free than other educators to exercise independent professional judgement. They pay the price for protecting the time and working styles of all other district officials.

3. The effects on handicapped children are positive; some benefit more than others.

The positive effects of PL 94-142 are of three kinds. First, state and local funding for education for handicapped children has grown markedly, in part as a result of local officials' eagerness to avoid litigation.

Second, "expensive" services (special placements for handicapped children who cannot be adequately served in district facilities) are available to parents who threaten litigation. Though school districts will not accede to all requests for expensive services, they readily grant those that are well founded in the law; parents also have at least an even chance to prevail if disputes are resolved through the due process system or in court.

Third, handicapped children who do not require expensive services often pay indirectly for the benefits won by litigants, as a result of reductions in the funds available for district-provided special education services. These losses are partly offset by the overall increases in funding for special education. But parents who have the strongest incentives to litigate can cause transfers of resources from other handicapped children to their own children.

A federal program that requires educators to use civil justice methods in allocating services changes school systems without requiring much action on the part of courts. School officials learn the applicable laws and take care to avoid mistreating beneficiaries.

- Thus, thanks to the introduction of civil justice methods, PL 94-142 is run with far more rigorous attention to the rights and duties of school personnel and beneficiaries.

PL 94-142 has had these effects without creating a large federal regulatory apparatus. Program regulations are a simple paraphrase of the authorizing statute, with a few amendments to reflect developments in case law. The federal monitoring and enforcement effort is much smaller for PL 94-142 than for other education-related civil rights laws and categorical programs. The federal Office of Special Education works to ensure that states maintain good due process systems. Federal officials have fewer direct contacts with local school officials under PL 94-142 than under other federal education programs.

These are optimistic conclusions, and none of our findings suggests that PL 94-142 should be amended to rely less on the civil justice system. However,

- Our findings do not necessarily warrant an extension of civil justice methods and assumptions to other areas of local educational policy.

The issues that arise in special education are particularly, perhaps even uniquely, well suited to resolution through judicial process. Furthermore, civil justice methods are unlikely to be efficient ways to make all of the trade-offs necessary for the management of all the services that school systems deliver.

SUITABILITY OF SPECIAL EDUCATION FOR MANAGEMENT BY CIVIL JUSTICE METHODS

Several characteristics of special education make it especially amenable to management through civil justice methods, including a premise of individualized entitlements; relatively small numbers of potential disputants; strong incentives for beneficiaries to complain about inequitable treatment; and efficient methods for characterizing disputes and remedies.

The basic premise of special education is that handicapped children differ from the children for whom schools are normally designed and that they require individually tailored educational services. Judicial processes are appropriate for the evaluation of individual cases. Because the principle of equitable treatment for handicapped children is widely accepted in society, disputes seldom involve major unresolved political issues.

Beneficiaries, especially parents, are well informed about their rights and have enough to gain from legal action to be willing to initiate it. Because the numbers of handicapped children are small relative to the whole school-age population, individual decisions can be made at moderate levels of administrative cost. Because professional standards for classifying children's needs and prescribing treatments are well developed, issues in controversy can be defined sharply. Most issues can be resolved in informal negotiations between beneficiaries and providers. When controversies come before courts, the issues and possible solutions are well defined.

Few, if any, other areas of local educational policy share these characteristics. Regular classroom instruction is aimed at the majority of students who are able to learn from group instruction and can make progress at a rate typical for children of their age. Although educators consider individual contact between student and teacher desirable, they do not believe that each child's instructional program could or should be individually tailored. "Categorical" education programs, like PL 94-142, are meant to help children who have special needs due to low family income, non-English-speaking background, or involvement in a desegregation plan. But those programs assume that children's needs are determined by their membership in a group: though individualized instructional programs may be useful, they are not a logical necessity, given the assumed source of the child's special needs.

The services provided by the categorical programs are expected only to complement regular classroom instruction. They are not assumed to be so valuable that needy students should receive them as a matter of individual right. The ESEA Title I program, for example, encouraged school districts to serve only a fraction of eligible recipients so that the effects of program funds on student achievement could be readily observed. In further contrast to special education, such programs also provide services that are of relatively little cash value: the annual per-student cost of most categorical program services is seldom more than $500 and never more than $1000.

Finally, no other categorical program has as finely developed a set of student diagnostic and treatment categories as does special education. It is, therefore, unlikely that categorical programs other than special education could produce disputes whose issues were as sharply defined, or whose remedies could be as efficiently described.[1]

---

[1] A concrete example will best make this point. In the case of *Lau v. Nichols,* 414 U.S. 563 (1974), the Supreme Court ordered school districts to provide appropriate instructional services to non-English-speaking children. On the surface, the principle established in that case resembles the "free appropriate public education" principle established by PL 94-142. But there are no good frameworks for assessing the needs of language-minority children whose home language is anything other than Spanish, and

UNSUITABILITY OF EXTENDING CIVIL JUSTICE METHODS TO THE MANAGEMENT OF OTHER EDUCATION SERVICES

PL 94-142 has been able to allocate its services through the civil justice system without creating enormous loads on the courts. It has succeeded in doing so for three reasons.

First, special education affects only a small portion of the elementary and secondary student population. The number of potential legal disputes, though large, is much smaller than it would be if all student placement decisions could be contested in court.

Second, the main types of special education are well established, and their standard uses are understood by both parents and providers. Therefore, the number of student placement decisions that produce serious misunderstanding or conflict between parents and school officials is low.

Third, special education funding has grown significantly since the enactment of PL 94-142. Services have improved across the board. Although, as we have found, parents who litigate successfully for expensive placements draw resources away from students who require only "standard" handicapped services, the size of the transfer thus created is not large. Had the transfers among handicapped students been more obvious, large numbers of parents might have initiated litigation to stabilize the quality of their children's services.

Imagine a different set of circumstances. Suppose that all students had legally enforceable service entitlements, rather than the 10 percent who are handicapped; that alternatives for student placement were poorly defined, so that conflict between parents and educators were frequent and hard to resolve; or that the transfers from nonlitigants to litigants were large and obvious, rather than small and hard to detect.

Under these conditions, the pool of possible litigants would be far larger than it is now; disputes would be less sharply defined and more difficult to resolve; and parents would have an incentive to use the courts to prevent transfers of resources from their children to others.

These circumstances could come about in special education if the definition of handicap is expanded to take in a wider range of students or if the transfers from the majority of handicapped children to the few who seek expensive services through legislation becomes more obvi-

---

no generally recognized alternative treatments. As Carpenter-Huffman and Samulon (1981) demonstrated, this problem is especially acute for children from Asian countries. For those children, disputes about their needs and entitlement would be difficult to formulate in a way that courts could settle without extensive inquiries into poorly defined technical questions.

ous. This outcome is unlikely, since local parent groups are now resisting efforts to broaden the definition of handicap and are discouraging their members from litigating for private gain.

If, however, legally enforceable entitlements were created for groups other than the handicapped, or if some general right to "appropriate services" were extended to all children, the consequences could be severe. If all students were able to establish their service entitlements through legal process, local education budgets would be allocated on the basis of a large number of independent legal actions. Since local budgets are not infinitely flexible, each case settlement would reduce funds available for all other students. Thus, all students in the district would be affected but not represented in disputes between individual parents and the school system.

If, as would be likely to happen, groups of parents filed class action suits to prevent transfers of resources from their children to others, the courts would ultimately be forced to make multilateral trade-offs among claimants. That process is essentially political, not judicial. It involves balancing competing claims, rather than the adjudication of particular rights. Though courts can certainly make some political decisions, there is no reason or need for them to replace the political processes through which school districts now govern themselves.

These considerations, we believe, would apply to any public service. If legally enforceable entitlements are established for large and diverse groups of people, the courts could become battlegrounds for interests that are now quite efficiently balanced through political processes. Entitlements effectively create advantages for small groups who would otherwise lose out in the competition for public services. But, a system in which everyone can use the courts to enforce a claim for individually tailored services will not work. The burden of arbitrating competing entitlements would overburden the courts and threaten their legitimacy without creating compensating improvements in the fairness or efficiency of public services.

REFERENCES

Carpenter-Huffman, Polly, and Marta Samulon, *Case Studies of Delivery and Cost of Bilingual Education,* The Rand Corporation, N-1684-ED, April 1981.

Cavanagh, R., and A. Sarat, "Thinking About Courts: Toward and Beyond a Jurisprudence of Judicial Competence," *Law and Society Review 14,* Winter 1980, pp. 371-420.

Gellhorn, Walter, Clark Byse, and Peter L. Strauss, *Administrative Law,* Seventh Edition, The Foundation Press, Mineola, New York, 1979.

Glazer, N., "Towards an Imperial Judiciary?", *The Public Interest,* No. 41, Fall 1975, pp. 104-123.

Hill, Paul T., *Enforcement and Informal Pressure in the Management of Federal Categorical Programs in Education,* The Rand Corporation, N-1232-HEW, August 1979.

Hill, Paul T., and Ellen L. Marks, *Federal Influence on State and Local Governments: The Case of Nondiscrimination in Education,* The Rand Corporation, R-2868-NIE, February 1982.

Hill, Paul T., and Richard A. Rettig, *Mechanisms for the Implementation of Civil Rights Guarantees by Educational Institutions,* The Rand Corporation, R-2485-HEW, January 1980.

Horowitz, D. L., *The Courts and Social Policy,* The Brookings Institution, Washington, D.C., 1977.

Kakalik, J. S., W. S. Furry, M. A. Thomas, and M. F. Carney, *The Cost of Special Education,* The Rand Corporation, N-1792-ED, November 1981.

Kimbrough, Jackie, and Paul T. Hill, *Aggregate Effects of Federal Education Programs,* The Rand Corporation, R-2638-ED, September 1981.

Kirp, David, William Buss, and Peter Kuriloff, "Legal Reform of Special Education: Empirical Studies and Procedural Proposals," 62:40 *California Law Review,* 1974, pp. 40-155.

Kirst, M. W., and K. A. Bertken, "Due Process Hearings in Special Education: An Exploration of Who Benefits" (mimeo), Stanford University School of Education, Stanford, Calif. 1981.

Meyer, J. W., *The Impact of the Centralization of Educational Funding and Control on State and Local Organizational Governance,* Stanford University, Program Report No. 79-B20, Institute for Research on Educational Finance and Governance, Stanford, Calif.,

August 1979.

National Institute of Education, *Administration of Compensatory Education,* Washington, D.C., 1977.

Rebell, M. A., "Implementation of Court Mandates Concerning Special Education: The Problems and the Potential," *Journal of Law and Education,* Vol. 10, No. 3, July 1981, pp. 335-356.

Silverstein, R., *An Introductory Overview Concerning the Basis for and Clarity and Restrictiveness of the Program Requirements Applicable to Local School Districts Applying for Grants under Title I, ESEA,* Lawyers' Committee for Civil Rights Under Law, Washington, D.C., 1977.

Stearns, M. S., S. D. Greene, and J. L. David, *Local Implementation of PL 94-142,* SRI International, Menlo Park, Calif., 1980.

Thomas, Margaret A., *State Allocation and Management of PL 94-142 Funds,* The Rand Corporation, N-1561-ED, September 1980.

Thomas, Margaret A., and Susan J. Reese, *Making Programmatic Decisions During a Time of Fiscal Retrenchment: The Case of Related Services for Handicapped Youth,* The Rand Corporation, N-1881-ED, July 1982.

Walker, W. E., J. M. Chaiken, A. P. Jiga, and S. S. Polin, *The Impact of Proposition 13 on Local Criminal Justice Agencies: Emerging Patterns,* The Rand Corporation, N-1521-DOJ, June 1980.

Wise, A. E., *Legislated Learning,* University of California Press, Berkeley, Calif., 1979.